SCHOLASTIC

READING

SATs TESTS

YEAR 5

SCHOLASTIC

Scholastic Education, an imprint of Scholastic Ltd
Book End, Range Road, Witney, Oxfordshire, OX29 0YD
Registered office: Westfield Road, Southam,
Warwickshire CV47 0RA

www.scholastic.co.uk

© 2019 Scholastic Ltd

123456789   9012345678

A British Library Cataloguing-in-Publication Data
A catalogue record for this book is available from the British
Library.

ISBN 978-1407-18306-0

Printed and bound by Ashford Colour Press

Author
Graham Fletcher

Series consultants
Lesley and Graham Fletcher

Editorial team
Rachel Morgan, Tracey Cowell, Anna Hall,
Rebecca Rothwell, Jane Jackson, Helen Lewis and Sally Rigg

Design team
Nicolle Thomas and Oxford Designers and Illustrators

Cover illustrations
Istock/calvindexter and Tomek.gr / Shutterstock/Visual Generation

Acknowledgements
Extracts from Department for Education website © Crown Copyright. Reproduced under the terms of the Open Government Licence
(OGL). www.nationalarchives.gov.uk/doc/open-government-licence/version/3/

The publishers gratefully acknowledge permission to reproduce the following copyright material:
Graham Fletcher for the use of 'Childhood in Victorian Britain', 'Buy a bike!', 'The Giant's Causeway', 'How to look after a rabbit', 'Cool
uniform', 'Gelert', 'Courageous animals', 'Hotel Blue Skies' and 'The Wreckers'. Text © 2015, Graham Fletcher. David Higham Associates
for the use of an extract from 'Boy – Tales of Childhood' by Roald Dahl. Text © 1984, Roald Dahl Nominee Ltd (1984, Jonathan Cape
Ltd). Ray Mather for the use of 'Two boys crying'. Text © Ray Mather 1996: www.raymather.co.uk
Every effort has been made to trace copyright holders for the works reproduced in this publication, and the publishers apologise for
any inadvertent omissions.

Illustrations: Moreno Chiacchiera, Beehive Illustration and Tomek.gr
Photographs:
Test A: Universal Images Group / SuperStock; © TopFoto; © The Keasbury-Gordon Photograph Archive/Alamy; © Topham Picturepoint;
        © Sergey Novikov/Shutterstock; © XiXinXing/Shutterstock; © Kanuman/Shutterstock; © Brian Goff/Shutterstock
Test B: © Graham Fletcher; © Concept Photo/Shutterstock; © Lucian Coman/Shutterstock
Test C: © PDSA; Lars Christensen/Photos; © RSPCA. The RSPCA helps animals in England and Wales. Registered charity no. 219099;
        © Rex/RupertHartley; © BMProductions/Shutterstock; © Elina/Shutterstock; © FamVeld/Shutterstock; © Sampien/Shutterstock;
        © Apelavi/Shutterstock; © THPStock/Shutterstock; LoloStock/Shutterstock; © Fotos593/Shutterstock

Contents
Reading: Year 5

About this book

This book provides you with practice papers to help support children with end-of-year tests and to assess which skills need further development.

Using the practice papers

The practice papers in this book can be used as you would any other practice materials. The children will need to be familiar with specific test-focused skills, such as reading carefully, leaving questions until the end if they seem too difficult, working at a suitable pace and checking through their work.

If you choose to use the papers for looking at content rather than practising tests, do be aware of the time factor. The tests require a lot of work to be done in 1 hour as they are testing the degree of competence children have – it is not enough to be able to answer questions correctly but slowly.

About the tests

Each Reading test consists of texts covering different genres and contains 50 marks. Each test lasts for 1 hour, including reading time.

- Reading texts: children may underline, highlight or make notes.
- Questions: children should refer back to the reading texts for their answers.

The marks available for each question are shown in the test paper next to each question and are also shown next to each answer in the mark scheme. Incorrect answers do not get a mark and no half marks should be given.

There are three different types of answer.

- **Selected answers**: children may be required to choose an option from a list; draw lines to match answers; or tick a correct answer. Usually 1 mark will be awarded.
- **Short answers**: children will need to write a phrase or use information from the text. Usually 1–2 marks will be awarded.
- **Several line answers**: children will need to write a sentence or two. Usually 1–2 marks will be awarded.
- **Longer answers**: children will usually need to write more than one sentence using information from the text. Up to 3 marks will be awarded.

Advice for parents and carers

How this book will help

This book will support your child to get ready for the school-based end-of-year tests in Reading. It provides valuable practice and help on the responses and content expected of Year 5 children aged 9–10 years.

In the weeks leading up to the school tests, your child will be given plenty of practice, revision and tips to give them the best possible chance to demonstrate their knowledge and understanding. It is important to try to practise outside of school and many children benefit from extra input. This book will help your child prepare and build their confidence and ability to work to a time limit. Practice is vital and every opportunity helps, so don't start too late.

In this book you will find three Reading tests. The layout and format of each test closely matches those used in the National Tests, so your child will become familiar with what to expect and get used to the style of the tests. There is a comprehensive answer section and guidance about how to mark the questions.

Tips

- Make sure that you allow your child to take the tests in a quiet environment where they are not likely to be interrupted or distracted.

- Make sure your child has a flat surface to work on with plenty of space to spread out and good light.

- Emphasise the importance of reading and re-reading a question, and to underline or circle any important information.

- These tests are similar to the ones your child will take in May in Year 6 and they therefore give you a good idea of strengths and areas for development. So, when you have found areas that require some more practice, it is useful to go over these again and practise similar types of question with your child.

- Go through the tests again together, identify any gaps in learning and address any misconceptions or areas of misunderstanding. If you are unsure of anything yourself, then make an appointment to see your child's teacher who will be able to help and advise further.

Advice for children

What to do before the test

- Revise and practise on a regular basis.
- Spend some time each week practising.
- Focus on the areas you are least confident in to get better.
- Get a good night's sleep and eat a wholesome breakfast.
- Be on time for school.
- Have all the necessary materials.
- Avoid stressful situations before a test.

What to do in the test

- The test is 60 minutes long. You should allow time to read the texts and then answer the questions.
- Read one text and then answer the questions about that text before moving on to read the next text.
- You may highlight, underline or make notes on the texts.
- There are 50 marks. The marks for each question are shown in the margin on the right of each page.
- Make sure you read the instructions carefully. There are different types of answer.
  - Short answers: have a short line or box. This shows that you need only write a word or a few words in your answer.
  - Several line answers: have a few lines. This gives you space to write more words or a sentence or two.
  - Longer answers: have lots of lines. This shows that a longer, more detailed answer is needed. You can write in full sentences if you want to.
  - Selected answers: for these questions, you do not need to write anything at all and you should tick, draw lines to, or put a ring around your answer. Read the instructions carefully so that you know how to answer the question.

Test coverage

Children will need to be able to:

- Give and explain meanings of words.
- Find and copy key details.
- Summarise main ideas from more than one paragraph.
- Use details from the texts to explain their thoughts about them.
- Predict what might happen.
- Identify and explain how information is organised.
- Show how writers use language to create an effect.
- Make comparisons.

Test A

Childhood in Victorian Britain

Life for children in the 21st century is full of electronics. Television and radio have been around for years but they have been joined by PCs, laptops, palmtops, the internet, texting, emails, online gaming, apps and a whole lot more. However, it wasn't always like this. A little over a hundred years ago, children's lives were very different.

It was easier for the rich

If you lived in Victorian Britain, your experience of life totally depended on whether you were born into a rich or a poor family. If you were rich, you had a privileged lifestyle, often in a large house with servants. If you were poor, you could expect to be working from the age of five or younger with little food or comfort.

Many died

In those days, many families had more than ten children. Very few of these would survive as poor diets, sanitation and health care led to a high death rate among young children. Fifty per cent of all recorded deaths were children under the age of five. Even the rich families were not immune to diseases like smallpox and measles.

The rich and the poor

It was easy to distinguish rich children from poor ones just by looking at them. Rich children had warm homes, were well fed, wore warm clothes and had shoes on their feet. They did not have to work and they either went to school or had tutors at home. Poor children were the opposite. They looked hungry and were thin. Their clothes would be tatty and they would be lucky if they wore shoes. Very few went to school as it was not compulsory for all until 1880. As a result of this, most children from poor families went to work.

Children at work

The vast majority of children were, of course, poor. Therefore their parents needed them to contribute to the family's income. Some children worked below the ground in coal mines. These were dark, dangerous places. The only light came from candles. Gas could choke the miners. Tunnels often flooded or collapsed, trapping the miners underground and often killing them. Young children usually did not dig for coal. Instead they pushed coal trucks around underground or opened and closed doors to let air in. In 1842, the government banned children under the age of ten from working in the mines. This age limit was raised to twelve in 1860 and later to thirteen in 1900.

In the factories

Other children worked in factories and cotton mills. Children worked in these places because they were small and could work in places that adults couldn't. They could get under the machines to pick up scraps of cloth. These children were known as 'scavengers', a word we still use today.

Toys

Victorian children did not have the advantage of television so their entertainment at home was very different to that of today. Plastic did not exist so toys were usually made of wood, metal, paper or card. Rich children would have factory-made toys but poorer children would have home-made ones.

Life was very different for Victorian children. Next time you go online, why not look up what it was really like for them?

Buy a bike!

So you want to buy a bike. It's a great idea! It gives you freedom, mobility and independence. What's more, it will keep you fit and healthy and save you money in the long run because you won't need to pay bus fares any more. So what's the catch?

There isn't one. It's just not as simple as it sounds. Before you buy a bike there are lots of things to consider, such as:

- what you want to use it for
- how much you can afford to spend
- where to buy it
- how you will maintain it.

What do you want to use the bike for?

This is really important because it determines the type of bike you need to buy. If you want to use your bike for riding to school, with your friends or around town, you won't want to choose the same kind of bike that you would if you wanted to perform stunt tricks on it. The four main types of bike that you are likely to choose from are:

- sporting bikes
- city bikes
- mountain bikes
- BMX bikes.

So what are the differences?

Sporting bikes look like racing bikes. They have drop handlebars and are lightweight. They have derailleur gears and thin tyres. The aim of these bikes is to go fast! They come into the category of road bikes but this is confusing as almost any bike that is meant to be used mostly on the road, as opposed to off-road, is a road bike.

City bikes are meant for use on the road but are very different to sporting bikes. These vary in appearance but a lot of them look like mountain bikes. They have stronger, heavier frames than sporting bikes and have wider wheels with thicker tyres that are designed to absorb bumps and pot-holes in the road.

Mountain bikes reflect their name. They are tough and rugged. They are designed for off-road use on paths, tracks and dirt roads. They can be used on ordinary roads but that is not their main purpose. Mountain bikes usually have suspension systems on the frame and the front forks. Their wheels are wide and their tyres are thick. They have powerful brakes and a large number of gears, particularly the lower ones to help their riders cope with steep hills and slippery conditions.

Finally, BMX bikes are completely different. They can be used on roads but they are designed to be used off-road in skate-parks or on home-made ramps and jumps. They can be used for BMX racing or 'Freestyle', where riders compete to perform the most difficult tricks they can.

You'll probably know already which type of bike you want but if you're not sure, ask for help in your local bike shop. To find your nearest stockist, look online.

How much do you want to spend?

It doesn't matter what type of bike you might want, you have to be able to pay for it. That means there will be inevitable compromises. You may have to accept a lower number of gears and a heavier frame to get the type you want. You may even need to give up on a type of bike completely because it is out of your budget. However, generally there are bikes covering a range of prices for all types. Expect to pay from about £100 for city or mountain bikes to thousands of pounds for carbon-framed racing bikes. Do some research before you buy to avoid disappointment. Everyone would like the most expensive, top-of-the-range models: few of us can afford them.

Where can you buy your bike?

It's up to you. You'll find bikes for sale in supermarkets and some department stores. There is plenty of choice online. However, for specialist advice and detailed knowledge, you can't beat being able to talk to someone at a recognised bike shop. They'll be able to help you with everything you need to know.

Maintenance

Check your bike over each week. Use a tyre gauge to find out the air pressure in the tyres and, if necessary, pump them up. Do a visual check on the tyres for signs of wear or damage. Test the brakes and make sure your gears are working. Unless you are handy with a spanner and a toolset, it is a good idea to have your bike regularly checked by an expert. It's not worth leaving things like brakes to chance! You know you are going to need them so make sure they work properly.

One last thing

So you've got your bike. Don't rush straight out on it. Remember to wear the safety equipment: helmet, gloves, reflective clothing and bright lights at night. Make sure you have a bell to warn other people of your presence and always carry a puncture repair kit. Get a strong lock to ensure your bike doesn't get stolen. Finally, always take great care when you are riding. You've got your dream bike. Make sure it doesn't become a nightmare.

The Giant's Causeway

IN IRISH MYTHOLOGY, Fionn mac Cumhail stands above all others. Perhaps this is not surprising as he was a giant who measured over fifty feet in height. In English, Fionn is known as Finn McCool – a very up-to-date name that unintentionally reflects his status in Irish folklore. In some versions of his story, he is not a giant but a hero with supernatural powers. In others, dating back to the third century, he is the leader of a group of warriors called the Fianna.

Legend has it that Fionn lived happily on the Antrim coast with his wife, Oonagh. One day, Fionn discovered that there was a rival giant living on the west coast of Scotland. Giants, by nature, are not friendly creatures. They do not trust strangers and are easily provoked. The appearance of another giant must have been seen as a threat by Fionn.

The Scottish giant, Benandonner, probably felt very much the same and it was not long before the two giants came to blows. It began, as fights so often do, with verbal insults. Fionn was frequently abused from across the sea by Benandonner, safe across the water.

Finally, Fionn could stand it no more. He clawed a huge lump of earth from the ground and hurled it with tremendous force across the sea in the direction of Benandonner. Was Benandonner worried by this? Not in the slightest. Why not? Despite all of the anger that Fionn put into his throw, the missile fell far short and landed in the Irish Sea, forming the Isle of Man. The hole that was made by Fionn digging out the earth filled up with rain water and became Lough Neagh in Northern Ireland.

All of this amused Benandonner no end and he laughed like a hyena, knowing that Fionn couldn't reach him. This was too much for Fionn who challenged Benandonner to a proper fight: man to man; face to face. Of course, Benandonner agreed. After all, a giant likes nothing better than a fight.

Benandonner might not have agreed so quickly if he had known what would happen next. Fionn started to build a huge pathway of enormous stepping stones so that he could cross the sea to Benandonner without getting his feet wet. For such bold and brave creatures, giants can be real softies sometimes.

When the walkway was completed, Fionn set off to meet his enemy. As he got nearer, Fionn realised just how big Benandonner was. Suddenly, fighting him didn't seem like such a good idea. It didn't take Fionn long to decide what he should do. Run!

He raced back home like an Olympic sprinter, closely pursued by Benandonner. Oonagh could see the fear in Fionn's eyes. She knew she had to do something so she dressed Fionn up as a baby and put him in a massive cradle. When Benandonner arrived, he did not see through the disguise. All he saw was a gigantic child and a smiling mother.

If the baby was that big, how big must the father be? Now it was Benandonner's turn to decide what he should do. Run!

He turned and fled back to Scotland. As he went, he ripped up large sections of the path to make sure that he couldn't be followed.

Is the story true? Certainly there are strange columns of basalt, a very hard rock, on the Antrim coast today. Legend has it that they are, in fact, the remains of Fionn's path and as a result are known as the Giant's Causeway.

Questions 1–13 are about *Childhood in Victorian Britain* on pages **8–9**.

Marks

1. Identify the **two** electronic devices that have been around for years.

1. _____

2. _____

1

2. Read the section headed ***It was easier for the rich***.
Find and **copy** a phrase that shows what your experience of life depended upon if you lived in Victorian Britain.

_____

_____

1

3.

> *Even the rich families were **not immune** to diseases like smallpox and measles.*

What do the words *not immune* mean in this context?

_____

_____

1

4. Give **two** reasons why it was easy to identify rich children just by looking at them.

1._____

2._____

2

5. Why did very few poor children go to school before 1880?

_____

_____

Marks

1

6. Read the section headed *Children at work*. **Find** and **copy** a phrase that shows that working in the mines was a risky occupation.

_____

_____

1

7. Where did the only light come from in coal mines?

_____

_____

1

8. Which of these did young children do in the factories?

Tick **one**.

Opened and closed doors to let air in ☐

Dug for coal ☐

Went under machines to pick up scraps ☐

Made toys ☐

1

9. Why were toys usually made of wood, metal, paper or card?

_____

_____

Marks

1

10. How does the final paragraph link back to the beginning?

_____

_____

_____

1

11. Look at the title of the passage: _Childhood in Victorian Britain._

Which one of the following would be the most suitable replacement for this title?

Tick **one**.

Working in a coal mine ☐

The differences between the toys of Victorian times and nowadays ☐

Rich and poor Victorian children ☐

Hard times ☐

1

12. Explain how the writer tries to make us feel sympathy for Victorian children, referring to the text in your answer.

_____

_____

_____

_____

_____

3

13. This passage was written to inform people about what life was like for Victorian children.

Give **two** features of the text that support this purpose.

I. _____

2. _____

1

Reading

Test A

> **Questions** 14–26 are about *Buy a bike!* on pages **10–11**.

14. According to the article, which of these is something to consider before you buy a bike?

Tick **one**.

The colour you would like most ☐

Where you will keep it ☐

How much you can afford to spend ☐

The kind of bike your friend has ☐

1

15. Look at the section headed ***What do you want to use the bike for?***

What are the **four** main types of bike that could be chosen?

1. _____

2. _____

3. _____

4. _____

1

Marks

16. Compare the uses of sporting bikes and BMX bikes. Give **two** examples of the differences between them.

_____

_____

_____

_____

2

17. Read the section headed *Maintenance*. How does the writer try to persuade the reader that it is a good idea to have bikes checked regularly by experts?

_____

_____

1

18. What is likely to happen if you do not get a strong lock for your bike?

_____

1

19. Tick the correct boxes to show whether the following statements are **facts** or **opinions**.

	Fact	Opinion
You'll find bikes for sale in supermarkets and some department stores.		
There is plenty of choice online.		
However, for specialist advice and detailed knowledge, you can't beat being able to talk to someone at a recognised bike shop.		

Marks

1

20. Which is the most likely intention of the article?

Tick **one**.

To persuade the reader to buy a sporting bike ☐

To inform bike buyers of the choices available ☐

To argue that young people should not buy bikes ☐

To compare bikes to other forms of transport ☐

1

Marks

21. Read these two sentences and use them to answer the questions below.

> *You've got your dream bike. Make sure **it** doesn't become a nightmare.*

a. What does the word *it* refer to in the last sentence?

_____

1

b. What idea links the two sentences?

Tick one.

Riding bikes ⬜

Being scared ⬜

Sleep ⬜

1

22. In the context of the final two sentences in the text, what do you think *nightmare* might mean?

_____

_____

_____

2

23. Give **two** reasons why you might expect the text of *Buy a Bike!* to appear in a magazine called *The best bike for you.*

I. _____

2. _____

2

24. How do the headings of each section help us to understand the text?

_____

_____

1

25. What is the main idea in the section headed *Where can you buy your bike?*

_____

_____

1

26. Identify **two** key details that support the main idea of the section headed *Where can you buy your bike?*

I. _____

2. _____

2

Marks

Questions 27–36 are about *The Giant's Causeway* on pages 12–13.

27. Use the text below to help you answer the questions.

Finally, Fionn could stand it no more. He clawed a huge lump of earth from the ground and hurled it with tremendous force across the sea in the direction of Benandonner. Was Benandonner worried by this? Not in the slightest. Why not?

a. Write down the word that shows how hard it was for Fionn to dig up the earth.

_____

1

b. Find and **copy** the phrase that suggests how little Benandonner was bothered by Fionn throwing earth at him.

_____

1

28. Which **three** land forms are supposed to have been created by Fionn?

I. _____

2. _____

3. _____

2

29. Why did Benandonner feel safe to shout abuse at Fionn?

_____

_____

Marks

1

30. According to the story, what do giants like nothing better than?

_____

_____

1

31. Explain how Oonagh tricked Benandonner and why he ran away.

_____

_____

_____

_____

2

32. Read this section about Benandonner.

> _He turned and fled back to Scotland. As he went, he ripped up large sections of the path to make sure that he couldn't be followed._

a. Identify a word that shows how scared he must have been.

_____

1

b. How did Benandonner try to stop Fionn chasing him?

_____

1

33. Number the following (1–5) to show the order in which they happen in the story. Number 1 has been done for you.

Marks

Benandonner was frightened and ran off home.	
The two giants shouted at each other across the sea.	
Fionn built a walkway.	
Fionn lived happily with his wife.	1
Oonagh hid Fionn.	

1

34. Why do you think both Benadonner and Fionn ran away from each other?

_____

1

35. Choose the **best word or group of words** to fit the sentences below and put a **circle** around your choice.

Marks

a. In some accounts of the story, Fionn is seen as a:

| bully | coward | hero | weakling |

1

b. Fionn ran home like:

the wind

an experienced jogger

a champion high jumper

a snail

1

c. The story could be true because:

the Giant's Causeway still exists

people still tell the story today

giants still live there

myths and legends are always true

1

■SCHOLASTIC National Curriculum SATs Tests

36.

> *Legend has it* that they are, in fact, the remains of Fionn's path.

Draw a line to show the phrase that is closest in meaning to *Legend has it*.

Legend has it

It is certain that

It is hoped that

It is not that

It is believed that

End of test

Test A Marks

Question	Focus	Possible marks	Actual marks
1	Information/key details	1	
2	Making inferences	1	
3	Meanings of words	1	
4	Information/key details	2	
5	Making inferences	1	
6	Making inferences	1	
7	Information/key details	1	
8	Information/key details	1	
9	Making inferences	1	
10	Identifying/explaining how information is related	1	
11	Making inferences	1	
12	Making inferences	3	
13	Summarise	1	
14	Information/key details	1	
15	Information/key details	1	
16	Making comparisons	2	
17	Identifying/explaining choice of words and phrases	1	
18	Predicting	1	
19	Making inferences	1	
20	Making inferences	1	
21	Identifying/explaining choice of word	2	
22	Meanings of words	2	
23	Making inferences	2	
24	Information/key details	1	
25	Information/key details	1	
26	Information/key details	2	
27	Information/key details / Making inferences	2	
28	Information/key details	2	
29	Making inferences	1	
30	Information/key details	1	
31	Information/key details	2	
32	Meanings of words / Information/key details	2	
33	Summarise	1	
34	Making inferences	1	
35	Making inferences	3	
36	Meanings of words	1	
	Total	**50**	

■SCHOLASTIC National Curriculum SATs Tests

Test B

How to look after a rabbit

Rabbits make great pets. They are affectionate, friendly and fun. However, looking after them can be complex. Don't be anxious though. Just follow the instructions below and you will have no problems.

Before getting your rabbit

1. Make sure you have the time to look after it.
2. Rabbits can be expensive to keep. Make sure you can afford it. You'll need to budget for the cost of the rabbit; somewhere to keep it; its food; and something to transport it in.

With all of that in mind:
- buy or make a hutch that is big enough for your rabbit. Remember baby rabbits grow!
- buy a carrying case that is sufficiently large to accommodate your rabbit but not too heavy to lift!

Every day

1. Ensure that your rabbit has enough to eat. Feed it on pellet food, hay and vegetables.
2. Change your rabbit's drinking water.
3. Play with your rabbit every day, especially if you only have one of them. Rabbits are sociable animals and need regular contact with you.

Every week

1. Clean your rabbit's hutch. Let's face it, your rabbit isn't going to do it. It's not a nice job but would you want to live in that mess? It's your responsibility so make sure that your rabbit has somewhere dry, warm and clean in which to live.
2. Change the straw that your rabbit uses for bedding. That way you'll keep your rabbit comfortable and also reduce the risk of infection and disease.
3. Give your rabbit some wood to chew on to stop its teeth becoming too long. Not all wood is suitable for rabbits, though. Check which ones are rabbit-safe first. Untreated pine is good.
4. Give your rabbit a check-up. Look for Red Eye. This is an unpleasant but common condition which causes irritation or swelling to the rabbit's eyes. If you see this, take your rabbit to the vet as soon as possible as it is often a symptom of a much more serious illness.

Every month

1. Check that the hutch is in good condition and repair any parts that need it. You may need some help with this. You'll also need to consider where your rabbit will stay while you are renovating its home.

Every six months

1. Take your rabbit to the vet to get an injection to prevent myxomatosis.

Other times

1. If you go on holiday, make sure you make alternative arrangements for the care of your pet. Get someone you trust to look after your rabbit while you are away.
2. If your rabbit starts to act differently or stops eating its food, take it to the vet straight away.

Now for the don'ts:

* Don't try to get it to do anything it doesn't want to do.
* Don't feed it light lettuce like iceberg.
* Don't feed it meat.
* Don't treat it as a toy.
* Don't ignore anything unusual in the way your rabbit behaves. This could be a sign that something is seriously wrong.

Follow this guide and you'll soon become accustomed to your rabbit. Very shortly you'll have lots of fun together.

Cool uniform

In the dim and distant past

The year is 1950: Pupils going to secondary schools have collected their new uniforms and are ready to set out on their first day. A last-minute check shows that the boys are wearing dark trousers, a white shirt, the school tie, a black blazer with the school badge on it and a cap. Girls are wearing the same except for a skirt instead of the trousers and a hat instead of a cap. All pupils are wearing sensible black shoes. They all have satchels, which are large leather bags, to carry their books in. They are all ready and can't wait to start!

Back to the future?

Fast forward to the present day: Pupils going to secondary schools have collected their uniforms and are ready to set out on their first day. So far so good. A last-minute check shows that the boys are wearing dark trousers, a white shirt, the school tie, a black blazer with the school badge on it. Wait a minute! Doesn't this sound familiar? What about the girls? It's almost the same! With very few variations, the uniforms that pupils will wear to go to their secondary schools will be almost identical to those of their grandparents! What's going on?

The times they are a-changing

Fashions have changed. In all other respects the clothes of today bear little resemblance to those of over half a century ago. Why is this not the same for school uniforms?

Or are they?

Caps and hats have almost disappeared and some schools have moved away from the traditional uniform to a more relaxed one. Ties seem to have been a major victim of what little change has taken place. They have been replaced in some schools by polo shirts and jumpers with the school badge on. These schools have usually ditched blazers as well. Very few secondary schools, have taken the brave step of doing away with uniforms completely.

SCHOLASTIC National Curriculum SATs Tests

Risky

Why would this be a brave move? Well, it seems that the main reason schools have uniforms is that parents expect them. The image of a school is formed by what people outside of it see of the pupils on the streets. If a school uniform is seen to be smart, the school is thought of in the same way and its reputation is improved. If pupils are seen to be scruffy...

Why? Why? Why?

Why haven't uniforms changed much over time? It's because they are what people expect to wear to school. The minor alterations, like the disappearance of caps and hats, reflect slight changes in our fashions but the reality is that uniforms haven't changed because very few people have seen a need for it. You go to school, you wear the uniform. End of story.

Where will it all end?

What would fashion designers like Gok Wan and Stella McCartney make of it all? Could they come up with something completely different that would please both pupils and parents alike? Something smart, distinctive and trendy. A cool uniform.

Gelert

Many years ago, legend tells us that Prince Llewelyn lived in a strong castle in the high mountains of North Wales. The prince was very brave and well respected by everyone. Proof of this was the prince's dog, Gelert, which was a gift from King John of England. One of the prince's favourite sports was hunting. Whenever he went hunting, Gelert went with him, always by his side or at the front of the pack. Gelert was a fearless friend and the prince trusted him completely.

Prince Llewelyn had known great sadness in his life. His wife had died giving birth to their son and the prince was broken hearted as a result of it. He promised his wife, as she lay dying, that he would love their son, look after him and protect him forever. Gelert loved the baby too and spent many hours sitting at the bottom of his cot, watching the child sleep, keeping him safe from harm.

Although the boy was only a baby, the prince knew that he would grow into a fine young man. It would not be long before the two of them would be able to ride together, hunting the wild boars, deer and other animals that lived in the deep Welsh forests in those days. Llewelyn looked forward to teaching his son to ride and to hunt.

In order to eat, the prince had to go hunting regularly. One day he was preparing to go out into the forest to try to catch some deer. He went to his young son's room to say goodbye. The baby lay in his cot, sleeping peacefully. Outside it was freezing cold but the room was kept warm by a huge fire and the baby had lots of thick covers over him. Llewelyn pulled his cloak tight around his shoulders as he headed towards the heavy wooden doors that led outside. Something made him stop. He had a feeling that all was not well. He could not say what it was but he felt something was not right.

The prince went back into his son's room. Everything seemed as it should be but still something troubled him. He made a decision. Today, Gelert would not hunt with him. Today, the dog would stay in the castle and look after the prince's baby.

"You are my most loyal, trusted and faithful friend. Look after him until I return tonight."

Llewelyn stroked the dog's hairy head and patted him on the back. Gelert's tail thumped gently on the floor and he lay down close to the cot, his eyes watching the sleeping child.

Many hours later, the prince returned. It had been a good day and he had caught lots of deer and a wild boar. There would be a huge party held that night to celebrate his success. Gelert did not meet him at the door but he was not surprised as he had told the dog to stay at his son's bedside and to protect him. That was where the dog would be.

The prince raced through the entrance hall like a whirlwind, eager to see both his son and his dog: the two things that mattered most to him in the world. He rushed into the baby's room and stopped in horror.

The sight that faced him filled him with fear and anger. The room had been wrecked. The thick covers on the bed were covered with blood. The boy's cot was overturned and the baby was missing!

Llewelyn could not move. He looked around the room and saw Gelert lying close to the cot. The dog got up slowly, walked to the prince and licked his hand. The prince looked into the dog's trusting eyes and saw the blood that covered its face. Instantly he knew what had happened. He had left the dog to protect his son and instead the dog had killed him!

Without hesitation, Llewelyn drew his sword and stabbed it through Gelert's heart. The dog dropped to the floor. His tail wagged weakly once and then he was still.

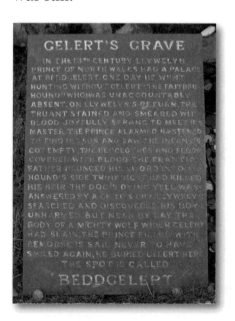

From behind the overturned cot, the prince heard a soft cry. The prince moved the cot to find his son, safe. Close by, he saw the body of a huge wolf, dead on the floor. He realised that Gelert must have saved his son, not killed him.

Llewelyn's joy at finding his son alive was matched by his despair for his dog. He ordered that the dog's body should be buried close to the castle, by the river, where he loved to walk. A large stone marks the spot and you can still see it today in the village of Beddgelert – Gelert's Grave.

Two boys crying

Across the world
Two boys are crying,
Both wanting more
And tired of trying.

The first boy wants a mountain bike
And blames his mum for being mean;
Had enough of the daily hike,
He's desperate to be part of the scene.

All day long
The wanting burns strong.
All the night
The wanting burns bright.
So little to ask,
Bikes are everywhere;
Oh, why is life so unfair?

The second boy wants something to eat
But is too weak to place the blame.
His mother weeps, helpless, dead-beat,
While his father hangs his head in shame.

All day long
The hunger burns strong.
All the night
The hunger burns bright.
So little to ask,
Food is everywhere;
Oh, why is life so unfair?

Across the world
Two boys are crying,
One's full of life,
The other is dying.

© Ray Mather 1996

Questions 1–7 are about *How to look after a rabbit* on pages **30–31**.

1. Why are rabbits great pets?

_____

_____

1

2. According to the text, what do you need to do before getting a rabbit?

Tick **three**.

Make sure you have time to look after it ☐

Take it to the vet ☐

Buy a hutch ☐

Watch it grow ☐

Buy one on holiday ☐

Buy a carrying case for it ☐

1

3. Read the section headed *Every week*. Referring to a condition called Red Eye, readers are told:

> *If you see this, take your rabbit to the vet as soon as possible as it is often a symptom of a much more serious illness.*

Give **one** other word or phrase that could be used instead of *symptom* in that sentence.

_____

_____

Marks

1

4. Read the section headed *Every month*.

What does *renovating* mean?

_____

_____

1

5. The following statements are either **fact** or **opinion**. Write the correct definition at the end of each statement.

Rabbits make great pets.   _____

Just follow the instructions below and you
will have no problems.   _____

Baby rabbits grow.   _____

Not all wood is suitable for rabbits.   _____

Very shortly you'll have lots of fun together.   _____

1

6. According to the article what should you do if:

a. you go on holiday?

_____

b. your rabbit starts to act differently?

_____

_____

7. Rabbits need lots of care.

Draw a line to match each **action** to its **purpose**.

Action	**Purpose**
Clean your rabbit's hutch	To prevent myxomatosis
Give your rabbit some wood to chew on	To stop the rabbit injuring itself
Check the hutch is in good condition	To stop its teeth becoming too long
Take it to the vet for an injection	To prevent disease and illness

Marks

1

1

1

Marks

Questions 8–17 are about *Cool uniform* on pages **32–33**.

8. a. What **six** items of clothing did boys wear to go to school in 1950?

1. _____

2. _____

3. _____

4. _____

5. _____

6. _____

1

b. Which **two** items of clothing are worn by girls but not boys?

1. _____

2. _____

1

9. The purpose of the article is to:

Tick **one**.

design new school uniforms. ☐

give the reader information about school uniforms. ☐

tell the reader which schools do not have school uniform. ☐

sell school uniforms. ☐

Marks

1

10. The article helps you to:

Tick **one**.

design your own uniform. ☐

choose schools to go to. ☐

know what life was like in the 1950s. ☐

understand why uniforms have not changed much. ☐

1

11. Read the section headed *Or are they?*

Which items of uniform have almost disappeared?

_____

1

■SCHOLASTIC National Curriculum SATs Tests

Reading

Test B

Marks

12.

> *These schools have usually **ditched** blazers as well.*

What does the word *ditched* mean in this sentence?

_____

_____

1

13. Give **two** reasons why it would be a brave move for schools to do away with uniforms.

1. _____

2. _____

2

14. Read the section headed **Why? Why? Why?**

Find and **copy** a phrase that shows why school uniforms have not changed much over time.

_____

1

Marks

15. Which **two** designers might be able to make different school uniforms?

1. _____

2. _____

1

16. The author seems to be against school uniforms in their present form. What evidence is in the article to prove this?

Give **three** pieces of evidence.

_____

_____

_____

_____

_____

3

17. Read the final sentence: *A cool uniform.*

a. Draw a line to join *A cool uniform* to the most likely meaning.

Marks

A uniform that is not warm

A uniform including caps and hats

A cool uniform

A uniform that is fashionable but not scruffy

A uniform that is cheap

1

b. Why do you think that the writer has used the word *cool*?

_____

_____

2

Marks

Questions 18–27 are about *Gelert* on pages **34–35**.

18.

> **Legend** *tells us that Prince Llewelyn lived in a strong castle...*

Draw a line to the type of story that is the closest in meaning to *Legend*.

Action story

Myth

Legend

Love story

Science fiction

1

---

19. What did Prince Llewelyn promise his wife he would do for their son?

_____

_____

1

20.

> *"You are my most loyal, trusted and faithful friend. Look after him until I return tonight."*

What does this tell us about the relationship between Prince Llewelyn and Gelert?

_____

_____

1

SCHOLASTIC National Curriculum SATs Tests

21. Why did the prince have to hunt for food?

Tick **one**.

The shops were closed ◯

He had a big appetite ◯

He needed food for Gelert ◯

In order to eat ◯

1

22.

> *The prince raced through the entrance hall like a whirlwind.*

This sentence contains:

Tick **one**.

a metaphor. ◯   alliteration. ◯

assonance. ◯   a simile. ◯

1

---

23. From the paragraph beginning *The sight that faced him filled him with fear and anger*, **find** and **copy two** things that might have made the prince think that something terrible had happened.

1. _____

2. _____

2

24. What is likely to have happened if Prince Llewellyn had not left Gelert with his son?

_____

_____

Marks

1

25.

> Llewelyn's joy at finding his son alive was **matched** by his despair for his dog.

What does the word _matched_ mean in this sentence?

_____

_____

1

26. Read the final paragraph. Explain why the story could be true, referring to the text in your answer.

_____

_____

2

27. Number the following (1–5) to show the order in which they happen in the story. Number 1 has been done for you.

The prince's wife dies.	1
The prince orders that the dog should be buried close to the river.	
Gelert kills the wolf.	
The prince finds the wolf.	
The prince goes hunting.	

1

Questions 28–36 are about *Two boys crying* on pages **36–37**.

28. What is wanted by the first boy?

_____

_____

1

29. What does the first boy think of his mother?

Tick **one**.

She is kind.   ☐

She has lots of money. ☐

She is mean.   ☐

She is poor.   ☐

1

Marks

30. The second boy is *too weak to place the blame.*

What does this tell us about the condition of the boy?

_____

_____

_____

2

31. Compare the things wanted by the two boys and why they want them.

_____

_____

_____

2

32. Which **two** things burn in the poem?

1. _____

2. _____

_____

1

33. How does the ending of the poem link back to the beginning of it?

_____

_____

2

34. What difficulties does each boy face?

First boy: _____

Second boy: _____

2

35. Find and **copy two** phrases that make the reader feel sympathy for the second boy.

1. _____

2. _____

2

36. Which of the following would be a good replacement for the title of the poem?

Tick **one**.

Life in England ☐

Life is so unfair ☐

Mean parents ☐

Happy birthday ☐

1

End of test

Test B Marks

Question	Focus	Possible marks	Actual marks
1	Making inferences	1	
2	Information/key details	1	
3	Meanings of words	1	
4	Meanings of words	1	
5	Making inferences	1	
6	Information/key details	2	
7	Information/key details	1	
8	Information/key details	2	
9	Summarise	1	
10	Summarise	1	
11	Information/key details	1	
12	Meanings of words	1	
13	Making inferences	2	
14	Making inferences	1	
15	Information/key details	1	
16	Making inferences	3	
17	Making inferences	3	
18	Meanings of words	1	
19	Information/key details	1	
20	Making inferences	1	
21	Making inferences	1	
22	Identifying/explaining choice of words and phrases	1	
23	Making inferences	2	
24	Predicting	1	
25	Meanings of words	1	
26	Making inferences	2	
27	Identifying/explaining how information is related	1	
28	Information/key details	1	
29	Making inferences	1	
30	Making inferences	2	
31	Making comparisons	2	
32	Information/key details	1	
33	Identifying/explaining how information is related	2	
34	Information/key details	2	
35	Identifying/explaining choice of words and phrases	2	
36	Summarise	1	
	Total	**50**	

SCHOLASTIC National Curriculum SATs Tests

Test C

Courageous animals

What is the PDSA?

If you have any pets, you will probably have heard of PDSA, or the People's Dispensary for Sick Animals. It is a major animal charity which cares for the pets of people in need, by providing free veterinary services to their sick and injured animals and encouraging responsible pet ownership. What you probably do not know is that PDSA also recognises the achievements of animals and gives awards for bravery by them.

The Dickin Medal

Maria Dickin, the founder of PDSA, established the PDSA Dickin Medal in 1943. It was to be given to animals showing great gallantry and devotion to duty while serving with British armed forces. The award is often regarded as the animals' Victoria Cross. The medal is made of bronze and has 'For Gallantry' and 'We also serve' inside a laurel wreath engraved upon it. Between 1943 and 1949 it was awarded 54 times, mostly to pigeons, for their work during and after the Second World War.

Up to May 2014, the PDSA Dickin Medal had been awarded 65 times.

SALTY AND ROSELLE

Some of their stories are quite remarkable. Salty and Roselle, two Labrador guide dogs, were caught with their blind owners in the World Trade Center terrorist attack, better known as 9/11. The two dogs remained loyally at the sides of their owners and bravely led them to safety down over seventy floors of the massive New York building.

BRIAN

Perhaps just as amazing are the exploits of Brian, an Alsatian. He worked with a Parachute Battalion of the 13th Battalion Airborne Division. He landed in Normandy in the Second World War and amazingly became a fully-qualified paratrooper.

The Gold Medal

The PDSA Gold Medal is the highest honour an animal can win in civilian life. It is the animals' George Cross. It too has a laurel wreath around the outside but the words inside it say '*For animal gallantry or devotion to duty*'. It is given to animals who risk their own lives to save the lives of others, or to animals killed or seriously injured while carrying out official duties in the face of armed and violent opposition.

The medal was first awarded in 2002. So far, all 23 of the animals to receive the award have been dogs. Their stories are no less amazing than those of the animals who have won the Dickin Medal.

DYLAN

Dylan worked with his handler as part of the Northern Ireland Search and Rescue Dog Association. In March 1999, four students were lost on the Mountains of Mourne, in Ireland. The weather conditions were atrocious but Dylan managed to find the group on a ledge 250 feet above ground level. The rescuers arrived shortly afterwards to lead everyone to safety. Later in the same year, Dylan worked in Turkey as part of the UK Fire Service Search and Rescue team and the International Rescue Corps following the earthquake in Turkey. He saved two people who were buried alive in the rubble after the massive earthquake. Dylan was awarded the PDSA Gold Medal in June 2006.

The PDSA is not the only body giving awards to animals. The Royal Society for the Prevention of Cruelty to Animals (RSPCA) recognised the bravery of a terrier in Bristol, who saved her owner when a bedside lamp fell onto her bed, the hot bulb setting it on fire.

It isn't just in this country that animal bravery is seen. In Australia, a kangaroo called Lulu received the RSPCA Purple Cross for saving the life of a farmer by alerting his family after he was knocked unconscious by a falling tree in a storm.

All around us, animals contribute to our daily lives. They are often taken for granted because they are part of our ordinary existence. They are the most wonderful friends we could possibly have. If only they could talk!

Hotel Blue Skies

To make paradise, you need to think out of the box. You need Blue Sky thinking. That's what we started with when we designed Hotel Blue Skies.

Basking beneath the azure Mediterranean sky, Hotel Blue Skies lies like a shimmering, sparkling jewel. Like its namesake, the hotel is heavenly. Cloud white buildings are surrounded by powder-blue pools and sea-green gardens.

Is it for you? A quick glance at the range of amenities Hotel Blue Skies offers will soon convince you!

ACCOMMODATION

Double rooms, all with sea views; Family rooms with garden views and plenty of space for everyone; Junior suites sleeping four people in luxury, including your own pool; Master suites sleeping up to six people, complete with ocean terraces and your own butler!

BARS

Eight bars including international and local specialities.

RESTAURANTS

Five 'eat as much as you want' buffet restaurants including Indian, Italian and Chinese.

POOLS

Seven pools including two kids' pools – one for the under-threes and one for the over-threes. All of the pools have water slides and one has a wave machine.

ENTERTAINMENT

Aerobics, archery, beach volleyball, tennis courts, mini golf, crazy golf, table tennis, fitness centre, yoga, three levels of kids' clubs. There are also Spectacular Staged Shows in the theatre every night and karaoke in the Sukiyama Bar.

SITUATION
Hotel Blues Skies is on a completely private island which can only be reached by boat – a wonderful, exciting and romantic way to start your relaxing holiday.
BEACHES
One adults only, three family beaches, one fun beach with boat hire and tours, canoes, banana boats and rings, pedaloes, para-gliding, diving lessons and wind-surfing.
PRICE
All-inclusive: £999–1599 per person, per week.

During the day you have an unrivalled choice of activities. You could while away your time on a luxurious lounger topping up your tan on the sun-kissed sand. If that sounds too slow for you, try the water sports on offer at the fun beach. That will set your pulse beating and raise your heartbeat. Alternatively, relax and be pampered in our fabulous Spa and Well-Being Centre where you will be waited on hand and foot – literally. For couples, why not enjoy a romantic walk through the pinewoods or a candlelit dinner on the beach?

There is something for everyone at Hotel Blue Skies. With our special all-inclusive offer there's no reason not to spoil yourself. Yes, it's true. Unlike some other hotels which limit you to certain brands and restaurants, absolutely everything at Hotel Blue Skies is included and unrestricted. You'll never have to say 'No' throughout your stay. What a wonderful present that would be for your loved ones.

Hotel Blue Skies is just a short plane flight away in distance but it's a whole world away in attitude. Surely you are worth the best, if only once. At Hotel Blue Skies, it need not only be once. Our prices and service will keep you wanting to return to this paradise year after year. Why not join us and experience for yourself the wonderful world of Blue Sky thinking?

The Great Mouse Plot

My four friends and I had come across a loose floor-board at the back of the classroom, and when we prised it up with the blade of a pocket-knife, we discovered a big hollow space underneath. This, we decided, would be our secret hiding place for sweets and other small treasures such as conkers and monkey-nuts and birds' eggs. Every afternoon, when the last lesson was over, the five of us would wait until the classroom had emptied, then we would lift up the floor-board and examine our secret hoard, perhaps adding to it or taking something away.

One day, when we lifted it up, we found a dead mouse lying among our treasures. It was an exciting discovery. Thwaites took it out by its tail and waved it in front of our faces. 'What shall we do with it?' he cried.

'It stinks!' someone shouted. 'Throw it out of the window, quick!'

'Hold on a tick,' I said. 'Don't throw it away.' Thwaites hesitated. They all looked at me.

When writing about oneself, one must strive to be truthful. Truth is more important than modesty. I must tell you, therefore, that it was I and I alone who had the idea for the great and daring Mouse Plot. We all have our moments of brilliance and glory, and this was mine.

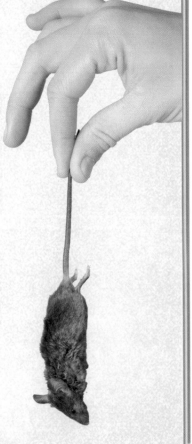

'Why don't we,' I said, 'slip it into one of Mrs Pratchett's jars of sweets? Then when she puts her dirty hand in to grab a handful, she'll grab a stinky dead mouse instead.'

The other four stared at me in wonder. Then, as the sheer genius of the plot began to sink in, they all started grinning. They slapped me on the back. They cheered me and danced around the classroom. 'We'll do it today!' they cried. 'We'll do it on the way home! *You* had the idea,' they said to me, 'so *you* can be the one to put the mouse in the jar.'

Thwaites handed me the mouse. I put it into my trouser pocket. Then the five of us left the school, crossed the village green and headed for the sweet-shop. We were tremendously jazzed up. We felt like a gang of desperadoes setting out to rob a train or blow up the sheriff's office.

'Make sure you put it into a jar which is used often,' somebody said.

'I'm putting it in Gobstoppers,' I said. 'The Gobstopper jar is never behind the counter.'

'I've got a penny,' Thwaites said, 'so I'll ask for one Sherbet Sucker and one Bootlace. And while she turns away to get them, you slip the mouse in quickly with the Gobstoppers.'

Thus everything was arranged. We were strutting a little as we entered the shop. We were the victors now and Mrs Pratchett was the victim. She stood behind the counter, and her small malignant pig-eyes watched us suspiciously as we came forward.

'One Sherbet Sucker, please,' Thwaites said to her, holding out his penny.

I kept to the rear of the group, and when I saw Mrs Pratchett turn her head away for a couple of seconds to fish a Sherbet Sucker out of the box, I lifted the heavy glass lid of the Gobstopper jar and dropped the mouse in. Then I replaced the lid as silently as possible. My heart was thumping like mad and my hands had gone all sweaty.

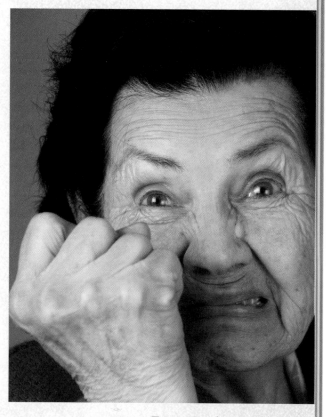

'And one Bootlace, please,' I heard Thwaites saying. When I turned round, I saw Mrs Pratchett holding out the Bootlace in her filthy fingers.

'I don't want all the lot of you troopin' in 'ere if only one of you is buyin',' she screamed at us. 'Now beat it! Go on, get out!'

As soon as we were outside, we broke into a run. 'Did you do it?' they shouted at me.

'Of course I did!' I said.

'Well done you!' they cried. 'What a super show!'

I felt like a hero. I *was* a hero. It was marvellous to be so popular.

From *Boy* by Roald Dahl

Along the south coast of England in the 19th century, 'wreckers' tried to trick ships into crashing onto rocks by shining false lights. Once the ships were wrecked, the wreckers then stole the cargoes.

The Wreckers

The sea was a bubbling furnace
and the wind an iron hand
that punched the ship in earnest
and drove it towards land.

The Captain saw a welcome light
and steered at its command.
He could not know that safety sight
was in a wrecker's hand.

Upon the rocks the ship did crash
with a sound of fearful thunder.
Across its bows the waves did lash
and tore it all asunder.

The wreckers hid in darkest night.
They could not hide their pleasure.
They watched the ship's pathetic plight
and waited for the treasure.

Upon the rocks the ship was tossed
till no more could be borne.
Crew and Captain all were lost:
no bodies left to mourn.

The treasure floated to the shore
and bobbed up on the beach;
Whisky, brandy, gold and more
within the wreckers' reach.

SCHOLASTIC National Curriculum SATs Tests

Then up the cliffs to hide the haul
and keep it safe from sight.
The church, the pub, behind a wall.
It must not come to light!

The soldiers came to the wreckers' lair,
an officer at their head,
and when he spoke, so soft and fair,
his words filled them with dread.

'Revenge I seek, that's why I came
and I will have no other.
The Captain and I shared a name.
He was my only brother.'

The soldiers then began their search
of anywhere quite handy
and in the altar of the church,
they found the gold and brandy.

They caught the wreckers one and all,
in twos and threes – the lot.
They were lined against a wall
and one by one were shot.

The soldiers left without a care.
The dead to them meant naught.
To those who ships tried to ensnare,
a lesson had been taught.

Yet still some try to tempt a ship
and take the plunder off it,
drawn by the treasure's fearful grip
and the wreckers' deadly profit.

Graham Fletcher (2015)

Questions 1–10 are about *Courageous animals* on pages **54–55**.

1. The PDSA has an important role in animal welfare. List **two** of its functions.

1. _____

2. _____

2

2. Why do you think so many pigeons received the Dickin Medal for their work during the Second World War?

_____

_____

1

3. Salty and Roselle were awarded the Dickin Medal because:

Tick **one**.

they were in the World Trade Center attack. ☐

they led their blind owners to safety after the 9/11 attack. ☐

they were Labrador guide dogs. ☐

1

4. What was amazing about Brian's achievement?

_____

_____

1

5. Why do you think the Gold Medal has been awarded fewer times than the Dickin Medal?

_____

_____

1

6. Give **two** reasons to explain why Dylan deserved his Gold Medal.

1. _____

2. _____

2

7. Which award was given to Lulu the kangaroo?

_____

1

8. Draw lines to match these words to their correct definitions.

gallantry		feats
devotion		dreadful
exploits		bravery
atrocious		dedication

1

9. Complete the table below using the following information.

Won by:
Animals in civilian life
Animals in the armed forces

Engraving on medal:
'For Gallantry' and 'We also serve'
'For animal gallantry or devotion to duty'

Medal	Won by	Engraving on medal
Dickin Medal		
Gold Medal		

1

10. a. Find and **copy** a word or phrase that shows the author's attitude towards animals that have won these awards.

Marks

_____

1

b. Explain how your word or phrase shows the author's attitude.

_____

_____

_____

1

Questions 11–20 are about *Hotel Blue Skies* on pages 56–57.

11. Read the **Accommodation** section.

a. What are the main features of Family rooms and Master suites?

Family rooms	
Master suites	

1

b. Compare what can be seen from Family rooms and Master suites.

_____

_____

1

c. What do Junior suites have that Double rooms do not?

_____

1

12. Where would you find karaoke?

_____

1

13. How does the information in the range of amenities table help the reader decide if Hotel Blue Skies is for them?

_____

_____

_____

_____

Marks

2

14. The article aims to persuade people to go to Hotel Blue Skies. How does it do this?

Tick **one**.

It says that it is really popular. ☐

It says it is easy to get to. ☐

It only says good things about the hotel. ☐

It says it is cheaper than anywhere else. ☐

1

15. Read the paragraph that starts _There is something for everyone._ **Find** and **copy one fact** and **two opinions**.

Fact _____

Opinion 1 _____

Opinion 2 _____

1

16. a. Read the final paragraph. **Find** and **copy two** phrases that would persuade people to go to Hotel Blue Skies.

1. _____

2. _____

2

b. Choose **one** of the phrases and explain why it would persuade people to go to Hotel Blue Skies.

Phrase _____

Explanation _____

_____

1

17. How does the ending of *Hotel Blue Skies* link back to the beginning?

_____

_____

2

18. Which devices in the article make it seem as if it is talking directly to the reader?

Tick **two**.

Repeating the words *you* and *your* ☐

Listing the entertainment ☐

Asking questions ☐

Repeating the words *us* and *our* ☐

1

19. Give **two** reasons why you think the hotel is called Hotel Blue Skies.

_____

_____

_____

2

20. When explaining the appeal of *Hotel Blue Skies*, the writer has deliberately chosen language that will have an effect on the reader.

Some of the words in the table below are in ***bold***. Explain the effect of these in each sentence.

Language used	Explanation of the effect of the language
Basking beneath the azure Mediterranean sky	
like a shimmering, sparkling ***jewel***	
the hotel is ***heavenly***	

3

Marks

> **Questions** 21–27 are about *The Great Mouse Plot* on pages **58–59**.

21. What **three** things did the five friends do every afternoon after the classroom had emptied?

1. _____

2. _____

3. _____

1

22. Why does the writer say *Truth is more important than modesty?*

_____

_____

1

23. a.

> We were tremendously **jazzed up**.

Replace *jazzed up* in the sentence with another appropriate word or phrase that will have the same meaning.

We were tremendously _____

1

b.

> We felt like a gang of **desperadoes** setting out to rob a train or blow up the sheriff's office.

Why do you think the friends felt like *desperadoes?*

_____

1

24.

> *We were the **victors** now and Mrs Pratchett was the*
> ***victim**.*

Marks

a. What do the words *victors* and *victims* suggest about why the boys wanted to play the trick on Mrs Pratchett?

_____

_____

1

b. Explain how the boys planned to trick Mrs Pratchett.

_____

_____

_____

1

25.

> *her small malignant pig-eyes watched us suspiciously as*
> *we came forward.*

a. Which word suggests that Mrs Pratchett is evil?

_____

1

b. Which word suggests that Mrs Pratchett does not trust the friends?

_____

1

26. Read the paragraph beginning *And one bootlace please.*
Find and **copy** the word that tells us how dirty Mrs Pratchett's fingers were.

_____

1

27. Number the following (1–5) to show the order in which they happen in the story. Number 1 has been done for you.

The five friends leave the shop.	
Thwaites orders a Sherbet Sucker.	
They decide to put the mouse into one of Mrs Pratchett's jars of sweets.	
Thwaites waves the mouse around.	
The five friends discover a secret hiding place.	1

1

Questions 28–33 are about *The Wreckers* on pages **60–61**.

28.

> *The sea was a **bubbling furnace**
> and the wind an **iron hand***

What do the metaphors *bubbling furnace* and *iron hand* tell you about the weather on the night of the wreck?

_____

_____

_____

_____

3

29. What happened to the captain and the crew in the shipwreck?

Tick **one**.

They all survived. ☐

Their bodies floated ashore. ☐

They were all killed. ☐

They were saved by the soldiers. ☐

1

Reading

Test C

30.

> *his words filled them with **dread***

Draw lines to link *dread* to **three** words with similar meanings.

dread

fear

happiness

joy

terror

alarm

delight

1

31.

> *Revenge I seek, that's why I came and I will have no other.*

What does this tell us about the officer who says it?

Tick **one**.

He is a fair man. ☐

He believes in law and order. ☐

He is only interested in revenge. ☐

He has come to look for the treasure. ☐

1

32.

> *The soldiers then began their search*
> *of anywhere quite handy*
> *and in the altar of the church,*
> *they found the gold and brandy.*

How does this verse link to the rest of the poem?

_____

_____

1

33. Read the final verse. What do you think is likely to happen next?

_____

1

End of test

Test C Marks

Question	Focus	Possible marks	Actual marks
1	Information/key details	2	
2	Making inferences	1	
3	Information/key details	1	
4	Information/key details	1	
5	Making inferences	1	
6	Information/key details	2	
7	Making inferences	1	
8	Meanings of words	1	
9	Information/key details	1	
10	Information/key details / Making inferences	2	
11	Information/key details / Making comparisons	3	
12	Information/key details	1	
13	Making inferences	2	
14	Making inferences	1	
15	Making inferences	1	
16	Making inferences	3	
17	Identifying/explaining how information is related	2	
18	Making inferences	1	
19	Making inferences	2	
20	Identifying/explaining choice of words and phrases	3	
21	Information/key details	1	
22	Making inferences	1	
23	Meanings of words / Making inferences	2	
24	Making inferences	2	
25	Meanings of words	2	
26	Meanings of words	1	
27	Summarise	1	
28	Making inferences	3	
29	Information/key details	1	
30	Meanings of words	1	
31	Making inferences	1	
32	Identifying/explaining how information is related	1	
33	Predicting	1	
	Total	**50**	

SCHOLASTIC National Curriculum SATs Tests

Marks & guidance

Marking and assessing the papers

The mark schemes provide detailed examples of correct answers (although other variations/ phrasings are often acceptable) and an explanation about what the answer should contain to be awarded a mark or marks.

Although the mark scheme sometimes contains alternative suggestions for correct answers, some children may find other ways of expressing a correct answer. When marking these tests, exercise judgement when assessing the accuracy or relevance of an answer and give credit for correct responses.

Marks table

At the end of each test there is a table for you to insert the number of marks achieved for each question. This will enable you to see which areas your child needs to practise further.

National standard in Reading

The mark that your child gets in the test paper will be known as the 'raw score' (for example, '22' in 22/50). The raw score will be converted to a scaled score and children achieving a scaled score of 100 or more will achieve the national standard in that subject. These 'scaled scores' enable results to be reported consistently year-on-year.

The guidance in the table below shows the marks that children need to achieve to reach the national standard. This should be treated as a guide only, as the number of marks may vary. You can also find up-to-date information about scaled scores on our website: www.scholastic.co.uk/nationaltests

Marks achieved	Standard
0–27	Has not met the national standard in Reading for Year 5
28–50	Has met the national standard in Reading for Year 5

Mark scheme for Test A (pages 7–28)

Q	Answers	Marks
1	**Award 1 mark** for radio and television.	1
2	**Award 1 mark** for 'your experience of life totally depended on whether you were born into a rich or a poor family' or 'whether you were born into a rich or a poor family'.	1
3	**Award 1 mark** for an appropriate explanation of the words *not immune* in this context. For example: • They could catch the diseases. • They were not protected against the diseases.	1
4	**Award 2 marks** for any two correct. Richer children: • were well fed • wore warm clothes • had shoes on their feet. **Award 1 mark** for one of the above.	2
5	**Award 1 mark** for answers that state that school was not compulsory for all till 1880. Or: most young children went to work. Also accept answers that refer to parents needing children to work.	1
6	**Award 1 mark** for any of the following: • These were dark, dangerous places. • Gas could choke the miners. • Tunnels often flooded or collapsed...	1
7	**Award 1 mark** for candles.	1
8	**Award 1 mark** for: Went under machines to pick up scraps	1
9	**Award 1 mark** for answers that explain that plastic did not exist.	1
10	**Award 1 mark** for answers that recognise the reference to technology or the repetition of 'very different'. For example: • It talks about going online to look up information and the first paragraph talks about PCs, laptops, palmtops, the internet, texting, emails, online gaming and apps. • The last paragraph talks about how life was very different for Victorian children. The first one says that a little over a hundred years ago, children's lives were very different.	1
11	**Award 1 mark** for: Rich and poor Victorian children	1

Q	Answers	Marks
12	**Award 3 marks** for an explanation that has at least three pieces of evidence from the text. Evidence could be a quotation or a reference to something in the text. Possible responses: ● The vast majority of children were poor. ● Poor children could expect to be working from the age of five or younger with little food or comfort. ● Poor diets, sanitation and health care led to a high death rate among young children. ● Fifty per cent of all recorded deaths were children under the age of five. ● Young children pushed coal trucks around underground or opened and closed doors to let air in. ● Poor children looked hungry and were thin. Their clothes would be tatty and they would be lucky if they wore shoes. Very few went to school. ● Even the rich families were not immune to diseases like smallpox and measles. **Award 2 marks** for an explanation that has at least two pieces of evidence from the text. **Award 1 mark** for an explanation that makes two points but does not support them with evidence from the text.	3
13	**Award 1 mark** for any two of the following: ● Photographs ● Headings/subheadings ● Information/facts about life in Victorian Britain ● The introduction is in bold	1
14	**Award 1 mark** for: How much you can afford to spend	1
15	**Award 1 mark** for all four correct: ● sporting bikes ● city bikes ● mountain bikes ● BMX bikes	1
16	**Award 2 marks** for a full answer that compares two uses of sporting bikes and BMX bikes. Possible responses: ● The aim of sporting bikes is to go fast. ● Sporting bikes are used on the road. ● BMX bikes can be used on the road but are designed to be used off-road in skate-parks or on home-made ramps and jumps. ● BMX bikes can be used for BMX racing or 'Freestyle' to perform difficult tricks. **Award 1 mark** for an answer that gives one piece of evidence or does not compare.	2

Q	Answers	Marks
17	**Award I mark** for answers that refer to any of the following: • Safety • To make sure the brakes and gears are working • You might not be able to do it yourself because you might not be good at maintenance/handy with a spanner and a toolset	I
18	**Award I mark** for responses that indicate that the bike may be stolen.	I
19	**Award I mark** for all correct:	I

	Fact	Opinion
You'll find bikes for sale in supermarkets and some department stores.	✓	
There is plenty of choice online.	✓	
However, for specialist advice and detailed knowledge, you can't beat being able to talk to someone at a recognised bike shop.		✓

Q	Answers	Marks
20	**Award I mark** for: To inform bike buyers of the choices available	I
21	**a. Award I mark** for the bike.	I
	b. Award I mark for: Sleep.	I
22	**Award 2 marks** for answers that refer to road safety or danger/accident and expand this by including references to the possibility of theft or injury. **Award I mark** for answers that refer to road safety or danger.	2
23	**Award 2 marks** for full answers with two reasons. For example: • The article is about bikes. • It tells you how to choose the right bike for you. • It tells you where to get advice on buying a bike. **Award I mark** for answers that include one of the above.	2
24	**Award I mark** for answers that indicate that they break the text up, making it easier to read. Or that they give summaries of each section.	I
25	**Award I mark** for answers that show that the main idea is that there are lots of places to buy bikes.	I
26	**Award 2 marks** for any two of the following: • You'll find bikes for sale in supermarkets and some department stores. • There is plenty of choice online. • For specialist advice and detailed knowledge, you can't beat being able to talk to someone at a recognised bike shop. **Award I mark** for any one of the above.	2

Q	Answers	Marks
27	**a. Award 1 mark** for clawed.	1
	b. Award 1 mark for: Not in the slightest.	1
28	**Award 2 marks** for all three of: ● Lough Neagh ● The Isle of Man ● The Giant's Causeway **or** the walkway **but not both**. **Award 1 mark** for any two.	2
29	**Award 1 mark** for answers that show that he knew that Fionn could not reach him.	1
30	**Award 1 mark** for a fight.	1
31	**Award 2 marks** for a full answer that includes: ● She dressed Fionn up as a baby and put him in a massive cradle. ● All Benandonner saw was a gigantic child and a smiling mother. ● Benandonner wondered if the baby was that big, how big must the father be? **Award 1 mark** for one correct reference to Oonagh and Benandonner.	2
32	**a. Award 1 mark** for fled.	1
	b. Award 1 mark for Benandonner ripped up large sections of the path or similar.	1
33	**Award 1 mark** for:	1

Benandonner was frightened and ran off home.	5
The two giants shouted at each other across the sea.	2
Fionn built a walkway.	3
Fionn lived happily with his wife.	1
Oonagh hid Fionn.	4

Q	Answers	Marks
34	**Award 1 mark** for answers that show they both realised how big each other was or they were scared of the size of each other or similar.	1
35	**a. Award 1 mark** for: hero.	1
	b. Award 1 mark for: the wind.	1
	c. Award 1 mark for: the Giant's Causeway still exists.	1
36	**Award 1 mark** for: It is believed that	1

SCHOLASTIC National Curriculum SATs Tests

Mark scheme for Test B (pages 29–52)

Q	Answers	Marks
I	**Award I mark** for answers that include: affectionate, friendly and fun.	I
2	**Award I mark** for all three correctly ticked: • Make sure you have time to look after it • Buy a hutch • Buy a carrying case for it	I
3	**Award I mark** for answers that include any of the following: indicator, indication, sign, warning, warning sign.	I
4	**Award I mark** for answers that include one of: repair, restore, mend, do up, decorate, fix up, spruce up.	I
5	**Award I mark** for all five correct. Rabbits make great pets. **Opinion** Just follow the instructions below and you will have no problems. **Opinion** Baby rabbits grow. **Fact** Not all wood is suitable for rabbits. **Fact** Very shortly you'll have lots of fun together. **Opinion**	I
6	**a. Award I mark** for make alternative arrangements or get someone you trust to look after the rabbits.	I
	b. Award I mark for take the rabbit to the vet straight away or take it to the vet straight away.	I
7	**Award I mark** for:	I

Action	Purpose
Clean your rabbit's hutch	To prevent myxomatosis
Give your rabbit some wood to chew on	To stop the rabbit injuring itself
Check the hutch is in good condition	To stop its teeth becoming too long
Take it to the vet for an injection	To prevent disease and illness

Q	Answers	Marks
8	**a. Award 1 mark** for answers that include all of: • dark trousers • black blazer • white shirt • cap • school tie • black shoes. **b. Award 1 mark** for answers that contain both of: • skirt • hat.	1 1
9	**Award 1 mark** for: give the reader information about school uniforms.	1
10	**Award 1 mark** for: understand why uniforms have not changed much.	1
11	**Award 1 mark** for hats and caps.	1
12	**Award 1 mark** for answers that indicate that schools have stopped using/got rid of blazers.	1
13	**Award 2 marks** for: • Parents expect school uniform. • The image of the school is created by the appearance of its pupils. **Award 1 mark** for either of the above.	2
14	**Award 1 mark** for either of the below: • they are what people expect to wear • very few people have seen a need for it.	1
15	**Award 1 mark** for Gok Wan and Stella McCartney	1
16	**Award 3 marks** for an explanation that has at least three pieces of evidence from the text. Evidence could be a quotation or a reference to something in the text. Possible pieces of evidence: • The uniforms that pupils will wear to go to their secondary schools will be almost identical to those of their grandparents! • What's going on? • Why is this not the same for school uniforms? • Very few secondary schools have taken the brave step of doing away with uniforms completely. • You go to school, you wear the uniform. End of story. • Could they come up with something completely different that would please both pupils and parents alike? • A cool uniform. **Award 2 marks** for an answer that has at least two pieces of evidence from the text. **Award 1 mark** for an explanation that makes two points but does not support them with evidence from the text.	3

Q	Answers	Marks
17	**a. Award 1 mark** for linking to: A uniform that is fashionable but not scruffy.	1
	b. Award 2 marks for answers that recognise the double meaning and the rhyming of cool and school for effect. The pupils may refer to puns but this is not necessary to gain both marks.	2
	Award 1 mark for answers that recognise the double meaning but do not comment on the rhyming of cool and school.	
18	**Award 1 mark** for: Myth.	1
19	**Award 1 mark** for: He would love their son, look after him and protect him forever.	1
20	**Award 1 mark** for answers that show that the prince trusts the dog. Possible responses: • The prince felt that the dog was loyal. • The prince trusted the dog completely. • The prince was happy to leave the dog to protect his son.	1
21	**Award 1 mark** for: In order to eat.	1
22	**Award 1 mark** for: a simile.	1
23	**Award 2 marks** for any two of the following: • The room had been wrecked. • The thick covers on the bed were covered with blood. • The boy's cot was overturned and the baby was missing! **Award 1 mark** for any answer that only includes one of the above.	2
24	**Award 1 mark** for answers that suggest that the boy would have been killed by the wolf.	1
25	**Award 1 mark** for answers that include: equal to, the same as, or similar.	1
26	**Award 2 marks** for a full answer that makes some inferences and uses evidence from the text to explain them. Possible responses: • Beddgelert is named after the dog. • There is still a large stone in the village where the dog is supposed to have been buried. • The stone can still be seen today. **Award 1 mark** for an explanation that implies some understanding.	2
27	**Award 1 mark** for:	1

The prince's wife dies.	1
The prince orders that the dog should be buried close to the river.	5
Gelert kills the wolf.	3
The prince finds the wolf.	4
The prince goes hunting.	2

Q	Answers	Marks
28	**Award 1 mark** for a mountain bike.	1
29	**Award 1 mark** for: She is mean.	1
30	**Award 2 marks** for answers that show understanding of the boy's physical and mental conditions. **Award 1 mark** for answers that only show understanding of one condition.	2
31	**Award 2 marks** for answers that include a mountain bike and food, and a comparison of them. This may include references to: ● the degree of need experienced by each child – one needs food to survive, the other is fed up of walking and wants to be 'part of the scene' ● the comparative expense of the food and mountain bikes ● other sensible comparisons. **Award 1 mark** for answers that only include a mountain bike and food.	2
32	**Award 1 mark** for both of: ● the wanting ● the hunger.	1
33	**Award 2 marks** for answers that recognise the similarity between the opening and closing lines and comment upon the differences. **Award 1 mark** for answers that recognise the similarity between the opening and closing lines.	2
34	**Award 2 marks** for ● First boy: his mother won't buy him a bike or he doesn't feel part of the scene because he hasn't got a bike, or similar. ● Second boy: has nothing to eat or is very weak or is hungry or similar. **Award 1 mark** for the correct answer to either part.	2
35	**Award 2 marks** for any two of the following: ● The second boy wants something to eat ● His mother weeps, helpless, dead-beat ● While his father hangs his head in shame ● One is dying **Award 1 mark** for any one of the above.	2
36	**Award 1 mark** for: Life is so unfair.	1

Mark scheme for Test C (pages 53–76)

Q	Answers	Marks
1	**Award 2 marks** for any two of: • Cares for the pets of people in need/provides free veterinary care. • Encourages responsible pet ownership. • Recognises the achievements of animals/gives awards for bravery. **Award 1 mark** for any one of the above.	2
2	**Award 1 mark** for any sensible answer. Answers do not need to be historically correct. Possible responses: • They were used to carry messages over dangerous land. • They risked getting shot at/injured while carrying messages. • More pigeons were used than other animals.	1
3	**Award 1 mark** for: they led their blind owners to safety after the 9/11 attack.	1
4	**Award 1 mark** for answers that include reference to him becoming a fully-qualified paratrooper.	1
5	**Award 1 mark** for any one of: • The Dickin Medal has been awarded since 1943, but the Gold Medal only started in 2002. • The Dickin Medal has been awarded for much longer. • Animals have to show great bravery to get the award. • Animals in the armed forces have more opportunities to show bravery and devotion. • Any other sensible answer.	1
6	**Award 2 marks** for: • He found lost students in atrocious weather. • He saved two people trapped in rubble after an earthquake in Turkey. **Award 1 mark** for one of the above.	2
7	**Award 1 mark** for the RSPCA Purple Cross. Accept Purple Cross by itself.	1
8	**Award 1 mark** for all correct: gallantry — feats devotion — dedication exploits — feats atrocious — dreadful bravery	1

Q	Answers	Marks
9	**Award 1 mark** for all correct:	1

Medal	Won by	Engraving on medal
Dickin Medal	Animals in the armed forces	'For Gallantry' and 'We also serve'
Gold Medal	Animals in civilian life	'For animal gallantry or devotion to duty'

Q	Answers	Marks
10	**a. Award 1 mark** for any of the following: • quite remarkable... • remained loyally... • amazingly became... • no less amazing... • any other justifiable answer.	1
	b. Award 1 mark for any of the following: • quite remarkable... shows that the author is full of admiration towards them. • remained loyally... shows that the author likes their devotion. • amazingly became... shows that the author sees this as very unusual and fantastic. • no less amazing... shows that the author thinks they deserve their medals as much as those who got the Dickin Medal. • other justifiable explanations.	1
11	**a. Award 1 mark** for a full explanation:	1

Family rooms	Family rooms have garden views and plenty of space for everyone.
Master suites	Master suites sleep up to six people, complete with ocean terraces and your own butler.

Q	Answers	Marks
	b. Award 1 mark for people in Master suites can see the ocean; people in Family rooms can see the garden.	1
	c. Award 1 mark for either: • luxury • your own pool.	1
12	**Award 1 mark** for Sukiyama Bar.	1
13	**Award 2 marks** for full answers that include any two of the following: • Provides a lot of information in a small space. • It tells them everything there is to do at the hotel. • It tells them the price. **Award 1 mark** for answers that refer to one of the above.	2
14	**Award 1 mark** for: It only says good things about the hotel.	1

Q	Answers	Marks
15	**Award 1 mark** for two correct opinions and one correct fact. **Opinions**: ● There is something for everyone at Hotel Blue Skies. ● There's no reason not to spoil yourself. ● Yes, it's true. ● You'll never have to say 'No' throughout your stay. ● What a wonderful present that would be for your loved ones. **Fact** (there is only one correct fact): ● ...absolutely everything at Hotel Blue Skies is included and unrestricted.	1
16	**a. Award 2 marks** for answers that include any two of the following: ● ...a short plane flight away in distance but it's a whole world away in attitude. ● Surely you are worth the best. ● Our prices and service will keep you wanting to return to this paradise year after year. ● ...experience for yourself the wonderful world of Blue Sky thinking? **Award 1 mark** for one of the above.	2
	b. Award 1 mark for an answer that explains why the phrase would persuade. Answers must be text-specific, for example: Phrase: a short plane flight away in distance but it's a whole world away in attitude. Explanation: This makes it seem like you can get there very quickly but you will find a different world when you get there. Do not accept answers such as 'It sounds like a nice place' or 'It sounds interesting'.	1
17	**Award 2 marks** for answers that recognise the similarity between the opening and closing statements and identify 'paradise' and 'Blue Sky thinking' as being repeated. **Award 1 mark** for answers that recognise the similarity between the opening and closing lines but do not include references to 'Blue Sky thinking' and 'paradise'.	2
18	**Award 1 mark** for both: ● Repeating the words *you* and *your* ● Asking questions	1
19	**Award 2 marks** for an answer that includes a reference to Blue Sky thinking and any one of the following: ● it is under an azure Mediterranean sky ● it is under a blue sky ● it has clear skies. **Award 1 mark** for an answer that includes: ● a reference to Blue Sky thinking.	2

20 **Award 3 marks** for three full explanations. 3

Language used	Explanation of the effect of the language
Basking beneath the azure Mediterranean sky	Basking sounds very relaxing. It makes the reader think of sunbathing. It makes the reader think of heat.
like a shimmering, sparkling **jewel**	Jewel makes it sound very valuable. It makes it sound very expensive. It makes it sound like treasure.
the hotel is **heavenly**	Heavenly makes it sound like paradise. It makes it seem peaceful and quiet.

Award 2 marks for two full explanations.

Award 1 mark for one full explanation.

Do not accept vague answers that are not text-specific, such as:
- it is a strong word
- it has a good effect.

21 **Award 1 mark** for answers that include all of the following: 1
- lift up the floor-board
- examine the secret hoard
- perhaps add to it or take something away.

22 **Award 1 mark** for answers that show an understanding that the writer is about to boast. 1

23 **a. Award 1 mark** for answers that show understanding that the boys were excited. 1

b. Award 1 mark for answers that suggest that the boys knew that what they were doing was almost like breaking the law. 1

24 **a. Award 1 mark** for answers that include one of: 1
- the boys had been treated badly by Mrs Pratchett
- the boys wanted revenge for something in the past.

b. Award 1 mark for answers that include two of the following: 1
- Thwaites would ask for one Sherbet Sucker and one Bootlace.
- Mrs Pratchett would turn away.
- The writer would put the mouse in the jar of Gobstoppers.

25 **a. Award 1 mark** for: malignant. 1

b. Award 1 mark for: suspiciously. 1

26 **Award 1 mark** for filthy. 1

SCHOLASTIC National Curriculum SATs Tests

Q	Answers	Marks
27	**Award 1 mark** for all five correct.	1

The five friends leave the shop.	5
Thwaites orders a Sherbet Sucker.	4
They decide to put the mouse into one of Mrs Pratchett's jars of sweets.	3
Thwaites waves the mouse around.	2
The five friends discover a secret hiding place.	1

Q	Answers	Marks
28	**Award 3 marks** for answers that analyse both 'bubbling furnace' and 'iron hand' to show the strength and ferocity of the weather. **Award 2 marks** for answers that analyse one of the metaphors to show the strength and ferocity of the weather. **Award 1 mark** for answers that describe the weather as being bad without analysing the metaphors.	3
29	**Award 1 mark** for: They were all killed.	1
30	**Award 1 mark** for all lines drawn correctly:	1

Q	Answers	Marks
31	**Award 1 mark** for: He is only interested in revenge.	1
32	**Award 1 mark** for answers that include any of the following references to earlier in the poem: ● The soldiers were there to find the treasure. ● The treasure had been hidden in the church earlier. ● The treasure included gold and brandy. Or answers that indicate that the verse makes references to events that have previously happened in the poem.	1
33	**Award 1 mark** for realistic answers that are linked to the final verse. Possible responses: ● The wreckers will continue to wreck ships. ● The soldiers will return. **Do not accept** answers that suggest that the wreckers will stop.	1

Notes

27 **Award 1 mark** for all five correct.

1

32 **Award 1 mark** for answers that include any of the following references to earlier in the poem:
- The soldiers were there to find the treasure.
- The treasure had been hidden in the church earlier.
- The treasure included gold and brandy.

Or answers that indicate that the verse makes references to events that have previously happened in the poem.

1

33 **Award 1 mark** for realistic answers that are linked to the final verse.
Possible responses:
- The wreckers will continue to wreck ships.
- The soldiers will return.

Do not accept answers that suggest that the wreckers will stop.

1

Notes

Notes